INCREDIBLY DISGUSTING FOOD

MYSTERY MEAT:
HOT DOGS, SAUSAGES, AND LUNCH MEATS

THE INCREDIBLY DISGUSTING STORY

Stephanie Watson

rosen publishing's
rosen central

New York

Published in 2011 by The Rosen Publishing Group, Inc.
29 East 21st Street, New York, NY 10010

First Edition

Library of Congress Cataloging-in-Publication Data

Watson, Stephanie, 1969–
Mystery meat: hot dogs, sausages, and lunch meats: the incredibly disgusting story / Stephanie Watson.—1st ed.
    p. cm.—(Incredibly disgusting food)
Includes bibliographical references and index.
ISBN 978-1-4488-1268-4 (library binding)
ISBN 978-1-4488-2284-3 (pbk.)
ISBN 978-1-4488-2288-1 (6-pack)
1. Sausages—Juvenile literature. 2. Frankfurters—Juvenile literature. 3. Meat—Health aspects—Juvenile literature. I. Title.
TS1974.S3W37 2011
664'.92—dc22

2010013649

Manufactured in the United States of America

CPSIA Compliance Information: Batch #W11YA: For further information, contact Rosen Publishing, New York, New York, at 1-800-237-9932.

CONTENTS

INTRODUCTION

The nineteenth-century Prussian/German politician Otto von Bismarck once said, "Laws are like sausages. It's better not to see them being made." The reason for his remark is that most people have no idea exactly what ingredients are concealed inside a sausage's casing—and they might not want to know. Are sausages filled with strange animal parts and nonmeat fillers? Are they loaded with artificial colors and chemicals?

Because of their dubious contents, sausages have been nicknamed "mystery meats." But sausages aren't the only meats that make people scratch their heads in wonder. Hot dogs, lunch meats, and canned meats also contain some questionable ingredients.

Not knowing exactly what ingredients are inside hot dogs, sausages, and lunch meats hasn't stopped people from eating a whole lot of these mystery meats. In 2009, Americans spent more than $1.6 billion on hot dogs and sausages in supermarkets, according to the National Hot Dog & Sausage Council. They also bought about 100 million cans of one popular brand of canned meat, the product's manufacturer reports. So what are mystery meats, anyway?

Sausages are one of the world's oldest processed foods. In *The Odyssey*, his epic poem that dates back to around the eighth century BCE, the Greek poet Homer described cooking sausages over a fire. Sausages are made from a combination of ground meat (usually beef, pork, lamb, and/or veal), bread, water, herbs, and spices. Colorings, preservatives (substances to keep the meat from spoiling), and salt are added. All of these ingredients are stuffed inside a thin outer shell called a casing. Natural casings are made from the intestines of cows, pigs, or sheep, or from a protein called collagen that is found in animal hides. Artificial casings are made from a plant-based plastic called cellulose. Sausages come in different varieties, which are based on their ingredients and how they are made. Bratwurst is a German pork sausage. Pepperoni is a spicy, dried Italian sausage that is made from beef and pork.

Hot dogs (also called frankfurters or wieners) are a variety of sausage that also have a long history. In 1987, the city of Frankfurt, Germany, celebrated the five hundredth birthday of the hot dog, which means the hot dog may have been around since the late 1400s. Hot dogs became popular in the United States in the 1870s, when German butcher Charles Feltman opened a hot dog stand in Coney Island, New York.

Hot dogs are usually made from beef or pork trimmings. Some varieties, though, have replaced these meats with chicken, turkey, or a meat substitute such as soy. The meat is cut up or ground into very small pieces. Then it is blended together in a machine with spices, preservatives, and salt to make a mixture called an emulsion. That mixture is stuffed into casings. Hot dog casings are usually made of cellulose, which is removed before the hot dogs are sold. Some hot dogs are made in natural casings, which are not removed. Finally, the hot dogs are hung up to dry in wood smoke in smokehouses to preserve them.

Canned meats are made from chopped, precooked pork or other meats. They are packaged with preservatives and other ingredients that help them last a long time on the shelf without spoiling.

Rounding out the mystery meats are the lunch meats, which include salami, bologna, ham, liverwurst, corned beef, and pastrami. Also known as cold cuts, these meats are sliced and usually served cold, often in sandwiches. Some lunch meats contain a combination of two different foods. For example, an olive loaf is bologna stuffed with olives.

Sausages, hot dogs, and canned and lunch meats have become very popular because they are inexpensive, convenient, and taste good. However, they aren't necessarily the best choices for a healthy diet. Sometimes, as Bismarck once noted about sausages, people don't want to know what ingredients are actually inside. If they did know just how much fat, salt, preservatives, and other chemicals were in the sausages, hot dogs, or canned meats they were eating, they might not want to take another bite.

WHAT'S IN YOUR HOT DOG?

In 1906, author Upton Sinclair wrote *The Jungle*, a novel that exposed the horrors of the meatpacking industry. In the book, he wrote, "There were things that went into the sausage in comparison with which a poison rat was a tidbit." Thanks in part to the furor that Sinclair's book caused, the meatpacking industry today is carefully regulated. As a result, sausages and hot dogs are far less mysterious and frightening than they used to be.

However, a lot of different ingredients are still stuffed inside a hot dog or sausage casing, and many of those ingredients aren't healthy. Fat, salt, preservatives, by-products, and fillers are all represented in large amounts, while many vitamins and nutrients are nowhere to be found.

By-Products and Fillers

Anyone who thinks they're eating the kind of meat they get in a hamburger or steak when they bite into a hot dog or sausage better think

Does this mixture look like meat? Workers at this beef factory are making hot dogs by combining a variety of fillers with other ingredients—just one of which is meat.

again. Sausages often contain meat by-products. These by-products can come from different parts of the animal, such as the muscle, heart, kidney, or liver. A hot dog can also contain meat from different animals combined (such as beef and pork), unless the label says "all beef" or "all pork." Turkey or chicken hot dogs might sound like healthier choices than beef or pork, but even they can contain some unsavory by-products, such as skin and fat.

Unappealing animal parts can also get into a hot dog when the meat is pulled from the animal. Hot dog manufacturers need to separate the cow, pig, turkey, or chicken meat from the animal's bones. A lot of the meat put in hot dogs is pulled from the animal using a process called advanced meat recovery (AMR). The meat is scraped, shaved, or pressed to remove it from the animal's bones without breaking the bones.

Another method for removing meat from bones is called mechanical separation. During this process, the animal's bones with the meat still attached are forced through a device under high pressure. The result is a batter or paste made from meat. Sometimes this meat paste can contain tissue from the cow's central nervous system (brain and spinal cord). Because of concerns over mad cow disease—a deadly brain disease in cows that can be passed on to humans through contaminated meat—mechanically separated beef is no longer allowed for use in hot dogs. However, hot dogs can contain up to 20 percent of mechanically separated pork and an unlimited amount of mechanically separated turkey and chicken. Any hot dogs that are made with mechanically separated meat must be labeled to inform consumers that they contain meat that was gathered in this way.

Sometimes meat isn't the only ingredient in hot dogs and sausages. Manufacturers also add cereal-filler ingredients, such as breadcrumbs, oatmeal, or flour, which help bind the meat together and add more weight to the product. Fillers tend to cost less than meat. The more fillers a company adds to its products, the more cheaply it can produce hot dogs and sausages.

Fat

Sausages and hot dogs contain fat—sometimes a lot of fat. Manufacturers are allowed to produce sausages that are as much as 50 percent fat, according to the U.S. Food and Drug Administration (FDA). Hot dogs can weigh in at up to 40 percent fat and added water.

According to government dietary guidelines, teens should get no more than 25 to 35 percent of their daily calories from fat. These guidelines recommend that most of the fat in a person's diet should be the healthy unsaturated kind, rather than the unhealthy saturated kind. (The difference between these two types of fat is explained in chapter 2.)

One hot dog can contain 13 grams (0.46 ounces) of fat or more, and 5 grams (0.18 oz) or more of that can be saturated fat. A single slice of salami is packed with 6 grams (0.22 oz) of fat, and half of that fat is saturated. Some large sausages can contain 20 grams (0.71 ounces) of fat or more! By eating just one hot

This brand of hot dog contains a whopping 11 grams of fat, including 5 grams of saturated fat. Just one of these hot dogs contains almost a quarter of the recommended fat intake for an entire day, according to the *Dietary Guidelines for Americans*.

dog or sausage, a person can get between 25 and 40 percent of the recommended fat intake for an *entire day*. Even chicken or turkey hot dogs can contain 8 or 9 grams (0.28 or 0.32 oz) of fat. Low-fat hot dogs are available, but they don't add much, if any, nutrition for the little bit of fat that was removed.

Pass the Salt

According to the American Heart Association, healthy adults should eat no more than 2,400 milligrams (1 teaspoon) of sodium (salt) each day. (People who have high blood pressure need to eat even less salt.) A single hot dog can contain up to 760 milligrams (0.03 oz) of sodium, and a thick slice of ham can contain more than 800 milligrams (0.03 oz). Eating just a few servings of these processed meats every day can put a person well above his or her daily salt requirement.

Chemical Preservatives

Hot dogs, sausages, and lunch meats such as salami and ham have a nice, rich red color to them. However, they didn't start out that way. Naturally, these meats would have a grayish color when cooked, similar to the color of cooked ground beef.

Because gray meat isn't very appealing to look at, manufacturers add the chemicals sodium nitrate and sodium nitrite. These preservatives not only add color to the meat, but they also prevent the meat from spoiling or being contaminated with the bacteria that can cause the dangerous disease botulism.

Hot Dog Ingredients

Most people have no idea what's really in their favorite hot dog. Here is a list of nonmeat ingredients found in some popular hot dog brands:

- Mechanically separated pork
- Corn syrup
- Sorbitol (an artificial sweetener)
- Dextrose (a type of sugar)
- Salt
- Sodium erythorbate (an additive)
- Sodium diacetate (an additive)
- Sodium nitrate and sodium nitrite
- Sodium phosphate (an additive that is also used as a laxative)
- Nisin preparation (a preservative made with bacteria)
- Red dye #40

Nevertheless, some health experts are worried that sodium nitrate and sodium nitrite aren't safe. These preservatives react with acids and other substances in a person's stomach to form chemicals called nitrosamines. In studies, nitrosamines have been found to cause cancer in laboratory animals.

Nitrates and nitrites are added to the meat during the curing process, which is the method of adding preservatives and smoking used to preserve hot dogs. Products that are labeled "uncured" do not have added nitrates and nitrites, although they aren't necessarily free from these ingredients. Nitrates and nitrites also occur naturally in some of the spices and other ingredients used to process even uncured hot dogs.

This magnified image shows *Listeria* bacteria. If a pregnant woman eats lunch meat that has been contaminated with *Listeria*, her unborn baby can get a dangerous infection called listeriosis.

Bacteria and Meat

When dry sausages are produced, salt and sodium nitrate are mixed with the meat to preserve it. Then bacteria are added to produce lactic acid, a chemical preservative that helps sausages last on store (or home) shelves for a long time without spoiling.

Usually the bacteria die at the end of the fermentation process. Sometimes, however, they can survive and make people who eat the sausage sick.

Sausages aren't the only mystery meats that can contain bacteria. *Listeria* is a type of bacterium that is normally found in the soil and water. When animals eat or drink food or water that is contaminated with these bacteria, the *Listeria* get into the animals' bodies. People who eat the meat that comes from these animals can become very sick if the meat isn't heated to a high enough temperature to kill the bacteria.

2 · · · WHAT MYSTERY MEATS CAN DO TO YOUR BODY

That hot dog or sausage eaten during a cookout or baseball game might taste delicious, but once that piece of meat makes its way through the body's digestive system, the trouble begins. Mystery meats are high in fat, sodium, preservatives, and other chemicals. In large enough amounts, all of these substances can wreak havoc on the body, leading to weight gain and a variety of diseases.

Big Fat Hot Dogs and Sausages

As discussed in chapter 1, hot dogs and sausages can contain 25 percent or more of a person's total fat requirements for an entire day. Adding these foods to a regular diet can increase total fat consumption. Because fat has more than double the calories of carbohydrates or protein, eating additional fat leads to greater weight gain.

Not all fats are created equal. Unsaturated fats, which are found in fish, nuts, and vegetable oils, are liquid at room temperature. This type of fat is considered healthy because it helps rid the body of cholesterol. (Cholesterol is an important part of the body's cells, but having too much of it in the blood can contribute to a disease of the arteries.)

Saturated fats, on the other hand, are solid at room temperature. Examples of saturated fats are cheese, butter, and the red meat found in hot dogs and sausages. Saturated fat raises the level of cholesterol in the blood, putting a person at risk for clogged arteries and heart disease.

The most artery-clogging kind of fat is trans fat, which isn't found in nature but is made in a manufacturing plant. Companies bubble hydrogen through vegetable oil at very high pressure and very high heat to make the oil thicker and more solid (products made this way are sometimes described as "partially hydrogenated" on their labels). The process of hydrogenation makes oil more stable so that food can be fried in it over and over again. It also gives foods an appealing taste and texture, and prevents them from spoiling. Trans fats also raise blood levels of unhealthy cholesterol and lower the levels of healthy cholesterol.

Artery-Clogging Cholesterol

Cholesterol is a waxy, fat-like substance that circulates in the bloodstream. Having some cholesterol is healthy because it's used to make the cell membrane—that outer layer of the cell—as well as some hormones.

Yet not all cholesterol is healthy. There is good cholesterol, and there is bad cholesterol. Bad cholesterol is known as low-density lipoprotein (LDL) cholesterol. This type of cholesterol is thick and sticky. It can build up on the inner walls of the arteries, much like food, hair, and other gunk can build up inside a sink drain. Eventually, the arteries can become so clogged that no blood can pass through them. The bad cholesterol forms a blockage that can cause a heart attack or stroke. Good cholesterol is called high-density lipoprotein (HDL) cholesterol. It acts like an artery cleaner, sweeping extra cholesterol out of the arteries to the liver, where it is removed from the body. This prevents cholesterol from clogging up the arteries and forming a blockage.

Hot dogs and sausages tend to be high in LDL cholesterol and low in HDL cholesterol. Eating too many of them can raise bad cholesterol levels in the body.

Salt Overload

Just as with cholesterol, salt (sodium) is fine to eat in small amounts. It actually serves a useful purpose in the body, keeping all of the

Cholesterol can collect in the arteries, forming fatty deposits called plaques. These deposits can eventually block blood flow through the arteries, which can lead to a heart attack or stroke.

body's fluids in balance, helping transmit nerve impulses, and making sure that cells, nerves, and muscles all work as they should.

The body has a system in place to ensure that sodium levels stay constant. When there is too little sodium, the kidneys—the body's filtering system—conserve sodium by putting whatever sodium the body doesn't use back into the bloodstream. Any time sodium levels get too high, the kidneys release the extra sodium into the urine to be removed from the body.

Yet even the hard-working kidneys can sometimes get overloaded. When someone eats a lot of high-salt foods such as hot dogs, potato chips, and pretzels, sodium starts to build up in the blood.

Sodium attracts and holds water (which is why a person who eats a lot of salt can feel like his or her body is more swollen or bloated than usual). Extra water ends up in the bloodstream, where it causes the total blood volume to increase. Blood pressure increases as a result. The heart has to work harder to push all of the extra blood through the body. Having high blood pressure can lead to heart disease and strokes (a blockage in the blood supply to the brain).

Do Hot Dog Preservatives Cause Cancer?

Sodium nitrite and sodium nitrate are two preservatives added during the meat-curing process. These preservatives help prevent the bacteria that cause botulism from forming, and they maintain the flavor and color of the meat. In the 1970s, some health experts raised concerns that sodium nitrite and sodium nitrate might also increase a person's risk for cancer.

In the body, proteins called amines can combine with nitrites and nitrates to form substances known as nitrosamines. There are many different kinds of nitrosamines, and most of them cause cancer in lab animals. Usually only a tiny amount of nitrosamines are formed in the body. The amount of nitrosamines formed depends on how the meat is processed, the length of time it is stored, and for how long it is cooked, among other things.

In a 2006 study published in the *Journal of Agricultural and Food Chemistry*, researchers took samples from hot dogs bought from the supermarket. When they mixed those samples with nitrites, nitrosamine compounds formed. These compounds had the ability to cause DNA mutations (changes). DNA mutations can lead to cancer. The researchers said DNA mutations in the gut that are caused by nitrates and nitrites could possibly increase a person's risk for colon cancer.

Even though there is some evidence that nitrites and nitrates might lead to changes in the body that increase the risk for cancer, there is no proof that hot dogs or any other mystery meats directly cause cancer. Health experts still consider these foods safe to eat in moderate amounts.

Colorful Meat

Food needs to taste, smell, and look good. Otherwise, no one would want to eat it. When meat is cooked, it might taste and smell good, but it isn't pretty. The natural color of a cooked hot dog is an unappealing gray. To make hot dogs a more appealing red color, sometimes manufacturers add man-made colorings, such as red dye #40.

Food manufacturers add dyes, such as this red dye #40, to their products to make them look appealing to eat. A number of health experts worry that some food dyes can cause health problems, including hyperactivity in children.

The big question is whether artificial dyes are safe for people to eat. At least one consumer group, the Center for Science in the Public Interest (CSPI), doesn't think they are safe. In 2008, it asked the FDA to ban the use of eight artificial dyes, including red dye #40. The CSPI says certain dyes make children hyperactive. Although there is no proof of this claim, there is evidence that removing dyes from the diets of children who have attention deficit hyperactivity disorder (ADHD) can improve the children's behavior. Yet the FDA still says food dyes are safe to eat.

Bacteria Bad Guys

Bacteria aren't always the bad guys. The body contains a lot of "good" bacteria, some of which live in the stomach and intestines and help with digestion. But sometimes, bacteria can make people sick.

Escherichia coli (*E. coli*) bacteria are both good and bad guys. They live in the intestines of humans and animals, and normally they're harmless. They even help the body make some important vitamins. Yet some kinds of *E. coli* produce a poison that can cause symptoms such as diarrhea and life-threatening problems that include kidney failure. Hot dogs and other meats that haven't been cooked properly can contain these dangerous *E. coli* bacteria.

Listeria is another bacteria bad guy. These bacteria can cause an infection called listeriosis, which is especially dangerous to pregnant women. It can cause the baby to be born too early or with very serious health problems. Heating meats until they are steaming hot can kill the bacteria that cause listeriosis.

Eating undercooked red meat that is tainted with *E. coli* bacteria, a cluster of which is shown here, can cause disease in humans. The signs of *E. coli* infection include intense stomach cramps, watery diarrhea that later can become bloody, and vomiting.

MYTHS AND FACTS

Myth: Hot dogs, sausages, and canned meats are called mystery meats because no one knows what's in them.

Fact: Mystery meats aren't really a mystery because the manufacturers are required to include nutrition labels, which state what ingredients are in the products. And, no, there aren't any really scary ingredients, such as ground-up rats or bugs. Everything that goes into a hot dog, sausage, or can of meat is considered by the U.S. government to be safe for humans to eat. However, that doesn't mean all of the ingredients are healthy.

Myth: Turkey and chicken hot dogs are healthier than beef or pork hot dogs.

Fact: Some turkey and chicken hot dogs might be lower in fat and calories than beef or pork varieties. Yet poultry hot dogs can still be high in salt, preservatives, and other unhealthy additives.

Myth: Hot dogs and lunch meats contain preservatives so that they can stay fresh forever.

Fact: Hot dogs and lunch meats can spoil quickly, especially once they're opened. Eating spoiled meat can make a person sick. Lunch meats need to be thrown out within three to five days of opening the package. Hot dogs stay fresh for only about a week once they are opened and refrigerated.

3 HEALTH EFFECTS OF EATING PROCESSED LUNCH MEATS

Just about every action that people take has at least one consequence. The consequence of eating a balanced diet and exercising is weight loss and overall good health. The consequences of eating a diet that is high in processed meats and other fatty foods include obesity, diabetes, heart disease, and cancer. No study has proved that mystery meats directly cause cancer or any other disease. Yet some research has found that these meats can increase people's risk for illness.

Weight Gain

Meat is high in fat. It makes sense, then, that eating a lot of meat can cause a person to gain weight. Studies seem to support this connection.

People who eat a lot of meat are 33 percent more likely to be obese and have extra fat around

One way that doctors determine whether their patients are overweight is by measuring waist circumference. People who have extra fat around their stomachs are at high risk for diabetes and heart disease.

their middle, according to a study published in the June 2009 issue of the *International Journal of Obesity*. Fat in the abdomen is the most dangerous kind of fat because it can increase a person's risk for heart disease, heart attack, and other dangerous diseases. The authors of the study say people whose diets are high in meat tend to have less room in their diets for healthy, low-fat foods such as fruits, vegetables, whole grains, and dairy.

Diabetes

Weight gain can also increase the risk for type 2 diabetes. Being overweight makes the body less sensitive to the effects of the hormone insulin. Normally, insulin helps move sugar from the bloodstream into the cells to be used for energy. When this hormone isn't working properly, sugar builds up in the bloodstream.

High blood sugar can cause a whole range of health problems, including kidney failure, nerve damage, and blindness. Eating a healthy diet and exercising to lose weight can help prevent or even reverse diabetes.

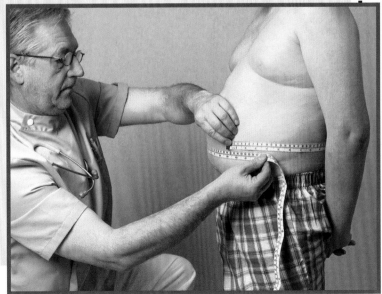

Heart Disease

Being overweight has yet another side effect. People who are obese are more likely to have heart disease, which can lead to a heart attack or stroke. Obesity boosts a person's heart disease risk by raising levels of unhealthy LDL cholesterol, lowering levels of healthy HDL cholesterol, raising blood pressure, and increasing the odds of developing diabetes (which is itself a risk for heart disease).

Researchers from the National Cancer Institute (NCI) studied five hundred thousand men and women and found that people who ate the most meat (1.5 ounces [42.5 g] of hot dogs, lunch meat, or other processed meats each day) faced the greatest risk of heart disease. Meat eaters were also at a greater risk of dying. Women who ate the most processed meats faced a 25 percent higher risk of dying, and men had a 16 percent higher risk, according to the study, which was published in a 2009 issue of the *Archives of Internal Medicine*.

A study published in May 2010 in the journal *Circulation*, found that eating just one serving of processed meats every day raised the risk of heart disease by 42 percent and diabetes by 19 percent. Unprocessed meats, such as beef and pork, didn't have any effect on heart disease. The authors of the study say the high sodium content in processed meats might be at least partly to blame for the increased heart risks.

That hot dog might taste good, but it can cause a lot of harmful effects in the body. Hot dogs and other processed meats can increase the risks for obesity, diabetes, and heart disease.

Cancer

The same *Archives of Internal Medicine* study found that eating meat, including processed meat, increased people's risk for developing cancer. The nitrites, nitrates, and other additives in hot dogs and other processed meats are believed to lead to the production of cancer-causing substances in the body.

After reviewing more than seven thousand large studies over five years, the American Institute for Cancer Research and the World Cancer Research Fund found that eating too much processed meat and being overweight increase the risk for cancers of the colon, kidney, pancreas, esophagus, uterus, and breast. For every 1.7 ounces (48 g) of processed meat (about the size of one regular hot dog) a person eats each day, the risk of colorectal cancer (cancer of the lower intestine and rectum) goes up by 21 percent.

A Pain in the Head

Migraines are very painful headaches that can also cause nausea, vomiting, and sensitivity to light. People who get migraines often have triggers—foods or other substances that seem to cause their headaches.

A migraine is a severe type of headache that can cause extreme pain, nausea, and eyesight problems. Certain preservatives and additives, including the nitrates and nitrites found in hot dogs and sausages, can trigger migraines.

Should Hot Dogs Come with Warning Labels?

A few studies have linked hot dogs and other processed meats with an increased risk for cancer. An organization called the Cancer Project believes that because of this risk, hot dogs should carry a warning label similar to the label on cigarette packages.

In July 2009, the Cancer Project filed a lawsuit in New Jersey asking that all hot dog packages sold in the state carry a warning label that reads, "Warning: Consuming hot dogs and other processed meats increases the risk of cancer." The hot dog industry has fought back, insisting that its products are safe.

The nitrates and nitrites found in hot dogs, sausages, and lunch meats are headache triggers for some people. The term "hot dog headaches" is used to describe migraines caused by these foods. Nitrites and nitrates are thought to cause headaches by widening the blood vessels in the head.

Breathing Problems

Health experts have known for years that smoking cigarettes and other tobacco products can lead to lung diseases. Now they've discovered that eating sausages, lunch meats, and other cured meats might also increase the risk.

A study printed in a 2007 issue of the *American Journal of Respiratory and Critical Care Medicine* found that people who ate cured meats at least fourteen times every week were 78 percent more likely to get chronic obstructive pulmonary disease (COPD) than people who never ate cured meats. COPD is a disease that is most common in smokers. It causes changes to the lungs that make it more difficult for a person to breathe. The authors of the study said the nitrates in cured meats might damage the lungs. People in the study who ate a lot of cured meats were also more likely to smoke tobacco products, which could also have caused the increased COPD risk.

When Mystery Meats Make People Sick

As mentioned in the last chapter, hot dogs and other processed meats can contain bacteria that can make people very sick. Listeriosis is an illness that can be caused by a type of bacterium found in lunch meats or under-cooked meat. While the meat is being transported, stored, or prepared, these bacteria can multiply and produce enough of themselves to cause infections in people.

In most healthy adults, listeriosis causes only mild flu-like symptoms, such as nausea, cramps, and diarrhea. In older adults, young children, or anyone with an immune system that doesn't work as well as it should, listeriosis can be very dangerous. Pregnant women who get the disease can lose their baby (miscarriage) or give birth too early (premature birth). To prevent illness, the Food Safety and Inspection Service of the U.S. Department of Agriculture (USDA) began testing sausages for *Listeria* bacteria in 1997. It also tests for *Salmonella*, another type of bacteria in undercooked meat that can make people sick.

E. coli are bacteria that can be found in undercooked meat (although they can also show up in healthy foods, such as spinach and other raw vegetables). In 1994, twenty children in the western United States became sick after eating dry-cured salami that was contaminated with E. coli bacteria. Three of the children were so sick that they had to go to the hospital. Parasites—tiny bugs that live off their hosts (including humans)—that can live in processed meats also cause illness. Trichinella spiralis is a worm that can live in undercooked pork (including the pork used to make sausages). People who become infected with these worms have symptoms such as fever, nausea, stomach pain, and vomiting.

Toxoplasma parasites are also found in undercooked meat or poultry. They cause the disease toxoplasmosis. In pregnant women, toxoplasmosis can cause miscarriage or health problems with the baby.

These are parasitic roundworms, Trichinella spiralis. The roundworm larvae live inside swine. People can become infected with roundworms when they eat undercooked pork. The parasitic infection is called trichinosis.

TEN GREAT QUESTIONS TO ASK A NUTRITIONIST

1: Can eating processed meats make me sick?

2: What kinds of illnesses are linked to processed meats?

3: Should I cut all processed meats out of my diet?

4: How much soda is too much to drink during a day?

5: Is it healthier not to eat any red meat (to become a vegetarian or vegan)?

6: How often is it safe for me to eat hot dogs and other processed meats?

7: Are the servings on hot dog, sausage, and lunch meat packages the right size for me?

8: How can I avoid getting sick from bacteria and parasites that can be found in processed meats?

9: What other foods should I eat to round out my diet?

10: How often do I need to exercise to keep at a healthy weight?

4

THE INGREDIENTS IN A HEALTHY DIET

Creating a healthy diet is a little like painting a picture. A painting that contains only one color is boring. By adding many different colors to their paintings, artists make their works interesting and appealing to the eye.

In much the same way, a diet that contains only one type of food is boring to eat. The way people add color to their diet is by eating a splash of fruits and vegetables; a dash of whole grains and dairy; and a sprinkling of meat, fish, and poultry. Hot dogs, sausages, lunch meats, and other processed meats can be a part of this colorful diet, but they shouldn't be the only color in it.

What You Should Be Eating

The USDA has established healthy eating guidelines, which make it easy for people to figure out how to build the perfect diet. The healthy diet

Cooking at home, instead of eating at fast food restaurants, is one way to ensure that you're eating a healthy diet. Fresh vegetables and fruits are a great addition to any diet. They're low in fat and high in nutrients.

pyramid (MyPyramid.gov) contains six food types: grains, vegetables, fruits, milk, meats and beans, and oils.

The healthiest types of grains are whole grains, which are given this name because they contain the entire grain kernel. Examples of healthy grains include whole-wheat bread, oatmeal, and brown rice. Teens should eat 5 to 7 ounces (142 to 198 g) of whole grains every day. One slice of bread or bowl of cereal counts as an ounce of whole grains.

Vegetables can be raw, cooked, or juiced. They cover all the colors of the rainbow, and it's hard to find one that's not healthy. Corn, green peas, broccoli, spinach, sweet potatoes, eggplant, green beans, squash, and onions are all good choices. Everyone should eat 2 to 3 cups of vegetables each day. Add 1 ½ to 2 cups of fruits such as apples, oranges, bananas, grapes, melon, and berries to complete the colorful mix.

The milk group includes not only milk itself, but also its dairy relatives, cheese and yogurt. People should aim to eat 3 cups of dairy each day. Low-fat or fat-free dairy products are the best choices.

Included in the meat group are chicken, turkey, fish, and beans. Teens should eat no more than 5 to 6 ounces (142 to 170 g) of meat every day, which is only a little bit bigger than a deck of cards. Hot dogs, sausages, and lunch meats are included in the meat group, but they should make up only a small percentage of the meat in a person's diet.

Healthier Alternatives

Not every hot dog or processed meat is created equal. Companies today make healthier varieties of these foods that are lower in fat, calories, salt, and preservatives. By choosing more nutritious options, people can eat lunch meats, hot dogs, and sausages once in a while without worrying that they will gain weight or add an unhealthy amount of sodium or preservatives into their diet.

Look for hot dogs and sausages that are low-fat or fat-free and low sodium. Turkey and chicken dogs may be lower in fat than beef or pork, but not always. When *Consumer Reports* tested several popular brands of chicken and turkey hot dogs in 2007, it found that most brands did have 30 to 80 fewer calories than beef or pork, but they were still high in fat and salt.

Vegetarian or vegan hot dogs and sausages tend to be lighter and healthier than meat or poultry because they are made with soy or another meat substitute. These products are naturally low in fat and cholesterol and high in protein.

Another option is to skip the processed meats entirely and eat a piece of lean beef, turkey, chicken, or fish, which are better sources of protein. The body needs protein to help it grow and for cells to develop.

To reduce the amount of nitrates or nitrates in their diet, people can choose natural "uncured" hot dogs. However, even natural products contain a small amount of these preservatives. Also, because they are uncured, natural hot dogs don't stay fresh for as long as cured brands.

Healthier lunch meat choices also exist. Chicken, turkey, or roast beef tend to be lower in fat and salt than ham, bologna, or salami. Some lunch meats come in low-sodium varieties. People who don't like the taste of low-salt meats can spread mustard on their sandwiches to add some flavor.

Some people may need to avoid certain processed meats altogether. Women who are pregnant are at a greater risk for contracting listeriosis and

FIGHT BAC!

Keep Food Safe From Bacteria

CLEAN
Wash hands and surfaces often.

SEPARATE
Don't cross-contaminate.

CHILL
Refrigerate promptly.

COOK
Cook to proper temperatures.

other infections and therefore should avoid eating hot dogs and lunch meats. Children under the age of three also need to be careful about eating these foods, especially hot dogs, which can pose a choking hazard. Anyone whose immune system doesn't work very well should heat any meat until it is steaming.

Safe Food Preparation

Hot dogs, sausages, and lunch meats are less likely to cause illness if they are prepared and stored safely. Most hot dogs are already cooked, but they should still be heated until they are steaming to prevent listeriosis and other infections caused by bacteria. People shouldn't leave hot dogs—even cooked ones—sitting out of the refrigerator for more than two hours (no more than one hour in

To prevent foodborne illnesses, meats need to be heated to their proper cooking temperatures. All food should be handled and stored correctly so that harmful bacteria are not transferred from one substance to another accidentally.

When you work out regularly, you don't have to count calories as carefully as someone who is overweight. Aim for at least thirty to sixty minutes of moderate exercise daily.

warm temperatures). To avoid getting sick, it's important to throw out any unused hot dogs within a week of opening the package. (Uncured hot dogs may need to be tossed out even sooner.)

Heat any uncooked meat sausages (those that contain beef, lamb, pork, or veal) until a cooking thermometer stuck in the middle reads 160 degrees Fahrenheit (71 degrees Celsius). Sausages that contain ground turkey or chicken should be cooked to 165°F (74°C). After handling raw meats, people should wash their hands in soap and water. They also need to clean any cooking surfaces that the raw meat touched.

When buying canned meats, look at the date on the can to make sure the food has not expired. Do not buy cans that are dented, cracked, or bulging. Clean the top of the can before opening it.

Everything in Moderation

Despite some of the warnings in this book, there is no need to fear or completely avoid hot dogs, sausages, lunch meats, or canned meats. People don't have to eliminate processed meats, but they should eat these foods in moderation. Eating a healthy diet made up of fruits, vegetables, whole grains, low-fat dairy, and lean meats makes it OK to indulge in a hot dog or sausage once in a while.

People who exercise regularly can feel even less guilt because they sweat off many of the calories they eat. According to government guidelines, people should aim for at least thirty minutes of walking, dancing, bicycling, weight training, swimming, aerobics, or other moderate-to-vigorous exercise every day.

Finally, it's important to be an informed eater. When people read package labels and food company Web sites, they know exactly what ingredients they're about to eat. They also know how much fat, salt, and nutrients are in their food. Being an educated consumer can take all of the mystery out of mystery meats.

GLOSSARY

botulism A type of food poisoning caused by *Clostridium botulinum* bacteria.

by-product Meat that comes from other parts of the animal, including the muscles, heart, kidney, or liver.

casing The outer covering of a hot dog or sausage, which is made from the intestines of a cow or pig, a protein called collagen that is found in animal hides, or a plant-based plastic called cellulose.

collagen A protein that is found in animal hides and is used to make the casings of hot dogs.

curing A process of smoking and adding salt and other preservatives to meat to help it stay fresh longer.

dubious Questionable or suspect; giving rise to uncertainty.

E. coli A type of bacterium that normally lives in the intestines. Some forms of *E. coli* can cause illness in humans.

emulsion A mixture of ground meat, spices, preservatives, and other ingredients that are blended together and stuffed inside a casing to make a hot dog.

fermentation The process of breaking down carbohydrates in organic substances by microorganisms; one of the oldest forms of food preservation.

filler Nonmeat ingredients that are added to hot dogs to give them more substance and weight.

high blood pressure An increase in blood volume in the arteries, which can force the heart to work harder and increase the risk for heart disease.

hyperactive A state in which a person is overly excited and has difficulty remaining calm.

Listeria A type of bacterium that can be found in lunch meats and hot dogs and can cause illness in humans.

mad cow disease A disease that affects the cow's nervous system. It can be passed to humans in contaminated meat.

nitrosamine A cancer-causing substance that can form in the body when it is exposed to nitrites and nitrates.

preservative A chemical added to food products to help them last longer without spoiling.

saturated fat An unhealthy type of fat that is solid at room temperature. Eating a lot of saturated fat can increase the risk for heart disease and obesity.

sodium nitrate/nitrite Chemicals that are added to processed meats to help them stay fresh for longer. Some health experts believe these preservatives can increase the risk for cancer.

stroke A blockage that prevents blood from flowing to an area of the brain. A stroke can damage the brain, leading to symptoms such as difficulty moving.

unsaturated fat A healthy type of fat that is liquid at room temperature. It helps clear cholesterol out of the arteries to prevent heart disease.

unsavory Disgusting or unappetizing.

vegan Someone who does not eat any animal or dairy products.

FOR MORE INFORMATION

American College of Nutrition

300 South Duncan Avenue, Suite 225

Clearwater, FL 33755

(727) 446-6086

Web site: http://www.americancollegeofnutrition.org

The goal of this organization is to promote education about proper nutrition.

American Dietetic Association (ADA)

120 South Riverside Plaza, Suite 2000

Chicago, IL 60606-6995

(800) 877-1600

Web site: http://www.eatright.org

The biggest organization of dietitians in the world, the ADA provides advice on healthy eating to help Americans make better food choices.

Canadian Council for Food and Nutrition

2810 Matheson Boulevard East, 1st Floor

Mississauga, ON L4W 4X7

Canada

(905) 625-5746

Web site: http://www.ccfn.ca

This organization helps Canadians gain a better understanding of food and nutrition issues.

Dietitians of Canada

480 University Avenue, Suite 604

Toronto, ON M5G 1V2

Canada

(416) 596-0857

Web site: http://www.dietitians.ca

This organization is made up of dietitians who promote better health through diet to the people of Canada.

National Hot Dog & Sausage Council

1150 Connecticut Avenue NW, 12th Floor

Washington, DC 20036

(202) 587-4200

Web site: http://www.hot-dog.org

This organization, which falls under the umbrella of the American Meat Institute, represents hot dog and sausage manufacturers.

Shaping America's Youth

120 NW Ninth Avenue, Suite 216

Portland, OR 97209-3326

(800) 729-9221

Web site: http://www.shapingamericasyouth.org

This group provides information about community programs across the United States that work to increase physical activity and improve nutrition among young people.

U.S. Department of Agriculture (USDA)

1400 Independence Avenue SW

Washington, DC 20250

(202) 720-2791

Web site: http://www.usda.gov

The USDA has several programs, including MyPyramid, that promote healthy eating, exercise, and other lifestyle habits.

U.S. Food and Drug Administration (FDA)

10903 New Hampshire Avenue

Silver Spring, MD 20993-0002

(888) 463-6332

Web site: http://www.fda.gov

The FDA is the government organization that ensures that food, drugs, and supplements are safe for the American public.

Web Sites

Due to the changing nature of Internet links, Rosen Publishing has developed an online list of Web sites related to the subject of this book. This site is updated regularly. Please use this link to access the list:

http://www.rosenlinks.com/idf/meat

FOR FURTHER READING

Armstrong, Dan, and Dustin Black. *The Book of Spam: A Most Glorious and Definitive Compendium of the World's Favorite Canned Meat.* New York, NY: Atria Books, 2007.

Claybourne, Anna. *Healthy Eating: Diet and Nutrition.* Portsmouth, NH: Heinemann, 2008.

Horowitz, Roger. *Putting Meat on the American Table.* Baltimore, MD: Johns Hopkins University Press, 2006.

Jones, Carol. *Sausage* (From Farm to You). New York, NY: Macmillan Library, 2007.

Kraig, Bruce. *Hot Dog: A Global History.* London, England: Reaktion Books, Ltd., 2009.

Martineau, Susan, and Hel James. *Meat, Fish & Eggs.* North Mankato, MN: Smart Apple Media, 2009.

Powell, Jillian. *Fats for a Healthy Body.* Portsmouth, NH: Heinemann, 2009.

Sylver, Adrienne. *Hot Diggity Dog: The History of the Hot Dog.* New York, NY: Dutton Juvenile, 2010.

BIBLIOGRAPHY

Allen, Gary, and Ken Albala, eds. *The Business of Food*. Westport, CT: Greenwood Press, 2007.

Bortolussi, Robert. "Listeriosis: A Primer." *Canadian Medical Association Journal*, Vol. 179, Issue 8, October 7, 2008, pp. 795–797.

Callaway, Ellen. "Steak and Hot Dogs Linked to Early Death." *New Scientist*, March 23, 2009. Retrieved January 31, 2010 (http://www.newscientist.com/article/dn16824-steak-and-hot-dogs-linked-to-early-death.html).

Center for Science in the Public Interest. "Protect Your Unborn Baby: Important Food Safety Information to Help Avoid Miscarriages." Retrieved January 31, 2010 (http://www.cspinet.org/foodsafety/brochure_pregnancy.html).

Choi, Charles Q. "Hot Dogs May Cause Genetic Mutations." LiveScience, August 14, 2006. Retrieved January 31, 2010 (http://www.livescience.com/health/060814_hot_dogs.html).

Consumer Reports. "Hot Dogs Without (Too Much) Guilt." July 2007. Retrieved January 31, 2010 (http://www.consumerreports.org/cro/food/resource-center/hot-dogs-7-07/overview/0707_dogs_ov.htm).

Cottrell, Charlie. "What's in Your Banger [Sausage]?" Interview with David Gardener. Channel 4 TV, January 23, 2009. Retrieved January 31, 2010 (http://www.channel4.com/food/features/what-s-in-your-banger-09-01-23_p_1.html).

Doheny, Kathleen. "Eating Red Meat May Boost Death Risk." WebMD, March 23, 2009. Retrieved March 22, 2010 (http://www.webmd.com/diet/news/20090323/eating-red-meat-may-boost-death-risk).

Hellmich, Nancy. "Put Down the Bacon! Report Emphasizes Cancer-Fat Links." *USA Today*, November 1, 2007. Retrieved March 22, 2010 (http://www.usatoday.com/news/health/2007-10-31-cancer_N.htm).

Hirsch, Jerry. "Hot Dogs Should Carry a Warning Label, Lawsuit Says." *Los Angeles Times*, July 23, 2009. Retrieved January 31, 2010 (http://articles.latimes.com/2009/jul/23/business/fi-hot-dog23).

Hodges, David. "Food Frights." *Today's Parent*. Vol. 19, Issue 4, May 2002, p. 56.

Jiang, Rui, David C. Paik, John L. Hankinson, and R. Graham Barr. "Cured Meat Consumption, Lung Function, and Chronic Obstructive Pulmonary Disease Among United States Adults." *American Journal of Respiratory and Critical Care Medicine*, Vol. 175, No. 8, April 15, 2007, pp. 798–804.

Johns Hopkins Bloomberg School of Public Health. "Diets High in Meat Consumption Associated with Obesity." September 3, 2009. Retrieved March 22, 2010 (http://www.jhsph.edu/publichealthnews/press_releases/2009/wang_meat_consumption_obesity).

Johnson, Megan. "Health Buzz: Processed Meats May Raise Heart, Diabetes Risk." *U.S. News and World Report*, May 18, 2010. Retrieved May 20, 2010 (http:// health.usnews.com/health-news/diet-fitness/heart/articles/2010/05/18/health-buzz-processed-meats-may-raise-heart-diabetes-risk.html).

Lapowsky, Issie. "'High-Fat Hangover': Eating Fatty Foods Lowers Memory Function in Brains, Bodies." *New York Daily News*, August 14, 2009. Retrieved February 2, 2010 (http://www.nydailynews.com/lifestyle/health/2009/08/14/2009-08-14_highfat_hangover_eating_fatty_foods_lowers_memory_function_in_brains_bodies.html).

Marie Claire. "Daily Sausage Cancer Risk." March 31, 2008. Retrieved January 31, 2010 (http://www.marieclaire.co.uk/news/health/201035/daily-sausage-cancer-risk.html).

Mirvish, Sidney S., James Haorah, Lin Zhou, and Marge L. Clapper. "Total N-Nitroso Compounds and Their Precursors in Hot Dogs and in the Gastrointestinal Tract and Feces of Rats and Mice: Possible Etiologic Agents for Colon Cancer." *Journal of Nutrition*, Vol. 132, Issue 11S, November 2002, pp. S3526–S3529.

National Hot Dog & Sausage Council. "Dachsunds, Dog Wagons and Other Important Elements of Hot Dog History." Retrieved January 31, 2010 (http://www.hot-dog.org/ht/d/sp/i/38594/pid/38594).

National Hot Dog & Sausage Council. "Factory Tour: How Hot Dogs Are Really Made." Retrieved January 31, 2010 (http://www.hot-dog.org/ht/d/sp/i/38596/pid/38596).

National Hot Dog & Sausage Council. "Vital Hot Dog Statistics." Retrieved May 21, 2010 (http://www.hot-dog.org/ht/d/sp/i/38579/pid/38579).

Ronzio, Robert A. *The Encyclopedia of Nutrition and Good Health*. 2nd ed. New York, NY: Facts On File, 2003.

Science. "Hot Dog Hazards." Vol. 264, Issue 5163, May 27, 1994, p. 1,255.

Sinclair, Upton. *The Jungle*. New York, NY: Doubleday, 2006.

Sinha, Rashmi, Amanda J. Cross, Barry I. Graubard, Michael F. Leitzmann, and Arthur Schatzkin. "Meat Intake and Mortality: A Prospective Study of Over Half a Million People." *Archives of Internal Medicine*, Vol. 169, No. 6, March 23, 2009, pp. 562–571.

SPAM.com. "Fun & Games." Retrieved March 1, 2010 (http://www.spam.com/games/facts/default.aspx).

U.S. Department of Agriculture. "Hot Dogs and Food Safety." Retrieved January 31, 2010 (http://www.fsis.usda.gov/Factsheets/Hot_Dogs/index.asp).

U.S. Department of Agriculture. "Sausages and Food Safety." Retrieved January 31, 2010 (http://www.fsis.usda.gov/FactSheets/Sausage_and_Food_Safety/index.asp).

U.S. Department of Agriculture. "Steps to a Healthier You." MyPyramid.gov. Retrieved February 2, 2010 (http://www.mypyramid.gov/index.html).

U.S. Department of Health and Human Services. "Dietary Guidelines for Americans 2005." Retrieved February 2, 2010 (http://www.health.gov/dietaryguidelines/dga2005/document/default.htm).

Zhou, Lin, James Haorah, Fulvio Perini, Steven G. Carmella, Takayuki Shibmoto, and Sidney S. Mirvish. "Partial Purification from Hot Dogs of N-Nitroso Compound Precursors and Their Mutagenicity After Nitrosation." *Journal of Agricultural and Food Chemistry*, Vol. 54, Issue 15, July 26, 2006, pp. 5,679–5,687.

INDEX

A

advanced meat recovery, 8–9

B

bacteria, and processed meats, 11, 13, 17, 19, 27–28, 33–34
botulism, 11, 17
breathing problems, 26–27
by-products, 8

C

cancer, and processed meats, 17–18, 22, 25, 26
cholesterol, 15–16, 24

D

diabetes, 22, 23, 24
dyes, in processed meats, 11, 18–19

E

E. coli, 19–20, 28

F

fat
    in processed meats, 10–11, 15
    saturated vs. unsaturated, 10, 15
fillers, 9
food pyramid, 32

H

headaches, 25–26
healthy diet, eating a, 30–36
heart disease, 22, 23, 24

L

Listeria/listeriosis, 13, 20, 27, 33, 34

M

mad cow disease, 9
meatpacking industry, 7
mechanical separation, 9

O

obesity, 22, 24

P

preservatives, in processed meats, 11–12, 13, 15, 17–18, 21, 25, 26, 33
processed/mystery meats
    health effects of eating, 22–29
    healthier versions of, 32–33
    ingredients in, 4, 5–6, 8, 9, 12, 13, 21
    limiting consumption of, 32, 36
    myths and facts about, 21
    popularity of, 4, 5, 6
    questions to ask a nutritionist about, 29
    safe preparation of, 34–35

About the Author

Stephanie Watson is an award-winning health and science writer based in Atlanta, Georgia. She is a regular contributor to several online and print publications, and she has written or contributed to more than two dozen books, including *Vitamins and Minerals*, *Fast Food*, *Trans Fats*, *Animal Testing: Issues and Ethics*, and *This Is Me: Facing Physical Challenges*.

Photo Credits

Cover, pp. 7, 14, 22, 30 John Block/Getty Images; cover (top) pp. 1, 4–5 © www.istockphoto.com/Sharon Dominick; pp. 8–9, 10 Scott Olson/Getty Images; p. 13 S. Lowry/Univ Ulster/Riser/Getty Images; p. 16 © B.S.I.P/Custom Medical Stock Photo; p. 19 © Bon Appetit/Alamy; p. 20 Photo by Eric Erbe, Colorization by Christopher Pooley/ars/usda; p. 23 Peter Dazeley/Photographer's Choice/Getty Images; p. 24 Chris Williams/Black Box/Lifesize/Getty Images; p. 25 Shutterstock.com; p. 28 Kim Taylor/Dorling Kindersley/Getty Images; p. 31 Comstock/Thinkstock; p. 34 http://www.fsis.usda.gov; p. 35 istockphoto/Thinkstock.

Designer: Les Kanturek; Editor: Kathy Kuhtz Campbell;
Photo Researcher: Amy Feinberg

ISBN 978-1-4488-2284-3
6-pack ISBN 978-1-4488-2288-1

rosen publishing's
rosen central